WILDLIFE
ON THE WATCH
A Story of the Desert

by MARY ADRIAN, *pseud*

Mary Eleanor Venn

Illustrated by Jean Zallinger

HASTINGS HOUSE · PUBLISHERS

NEW YORK

LIBRARY OF CONGRESS CATALOGING IN PUBLICATION DATA
Adrian, Mary, 1908-   Wildlife on the watch.
    SUMMARY: Describes the activities of a variety of birds, reptiles,
and mammals during one day in the southwest desert, with emphasis
on their interaction and territorial behavior.
    1. Desert ecology—Juvenile literature. 2. Territoriality (Zoology)—
Juvenile literature. [1. Desert animals. 2. Desert ecology. 3. Ecology.
4. Territoriality (Zoology)] I. Zallinger, Jean Day, illus. II. Title.
QH541.5.D4A37   596'.05'265   74-16167
ISBN 0-8038-1553-0

Published simultaneously in Canada by
Saunders of Toronto, Ltd., Don Mills, Ontario
Printed in the United States of America

FOREWORD

WHAT is a desert? Is it just miles of sand and cacti? Is it the silent, barren home of a few sleepy lizards?

That's what many people imagine. But, in fact, the desert of the American southwest is the home of a fascinating variety of birds, mammals and reptiles who live among many plants that have adapted to the dry climate.

Survival for the animals who make their home in this harsh environment is not easy. They struggle to find food and water. They are constantly on the watch for enemies. Many creatures eat animals of different kinds and are themselves eaten by still others. Owls eat snakes, snakes eat lizards, and lizards eat insects. And there is still another kind of rivalry on the desert. It is the fight for territory that takes place between members of the same species.

Many desert creatures claim territories. Usually it is the male animal that stakes out an area of land. On it he makes his home and hunts for food. He protects this land against other males of his species and tries to drive them away if they trespass. This struggle for territory helps prevent overcrowding.

At one time scientists thought that a bird sang to attract a mate. Now they believe that a bird also sings to warn other males that he is guarding the territory where he and his mate will raise their young. A woodpecker can't sing, but he advertises to other male woodpeckers that he is the owner of his territory by drumming on hollow trees.

Most mammals post their territories by smells rather than sounds. To warn trespassers away, a coyote urinates at certain regular stations on the outskirts of his territory. A jackrabbit leaves a small pile of droppings at sites on his home range. A kangaroo rat rubs the scent gland between his shoulders against bushes and trunks of trees.

Scientists have also observed that certain lizards establish territories. They leave scent tracks in the sand and attack male lizards who trespass on their feeding grounds.

From sunrise to sunset and through the night, the desert is alive with activity. This book follows some of the animals of the Arizona Sonoran desert as they hunt, mate, battle enemies and defend their territories. It tells, too, of the plants that play an important part in the interaction of living things.

I hope that you will want to read more about desert wildlife and that you will be interested in pursuing the subject of territorial behavior in other realms of the animal kingdom.

Portland, Oregon   Mary Adrian

California

ARIZONA

New Mexico

Mexico

1

SCENT STATIONS

A COYOTE watched the sun rising between two mountain peaks on the Arizona Sonoran desert. It cast an orange glow over a sandy stretch of ground.

Spring wild flowers nodded their petals in the cool morning breeze. And long shadows of saguaro cacti fell on the sand.

Coyote felt the urge to sing. He threw back his head and let out a long mournful howl, ending with several sharp barks.

After that there was silence. Not for long, though. A dove greeted the day with a cooing sound and a mockingbird sang his song. They were joined by more birds giving their musical calls.

Soon lizards, snakes and other daytime animals came out of burrows and hiding places, and began hunting for something to eat.

Coyote had spent the night hunting, but now he had to bring more food to his mate who was nursing their two-week old pups in the den. Eyes and ears alert for prey, Coyote moved slowly across the desert floor, his yellowish-grey fur blending with the color of the sand.

When he came to a paloverde tree with yellow flowers, he stopped and carefully sniffed the trunk. The tree was one of the scent stations on his territory.

Coyote had his own special hunting ground. He guarded it from other male coyotes. In this way, there would be enough food for him and his family. He marked the boundaries of his territory by urinating on rocks, stumps, bushes and trees like this paloverde.

His scent would warn any strange coyote that he was on the edge of another's territory. Coyote sniffed the tree to see if his scent was still strong enough.

Then he left a fresh urine odor on the paloverde trunk to warn strangers away. After that
he moved on, looking for a ground squirrel or a
mouse to catch.

Presently he came to an ocotillo bush tipped
with red flowers. This was another scent station.
Coyote sniffed vigorously at it. The odor told
him plenty. Another male coyote had come into
his territory.

Coyote was disturbed. Hair standing on end, he growled and scratched the ground around the ocotillo with his hind feet. Then he walked off, looking back from time to time.

It was not long before Coyote spotted the trespasser. He was an old male, and the intruder knew that he had crossed into foreign territory. He saw Coyote heading toward him, but he made no effort to leave.

Hair bristling, Coyote rushed up to the stranger.

They met head-on, each one trying to snap at the other's throat. Snarling, they backed away. Then, like a streak of lightning, Coyote rushed in and bit the old male in the foreleg.

The trespasser let out a loud yelp. Slowly, he limped away.

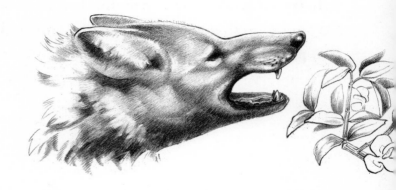

Coyote followed him to the end of his territory growling and baring his teeth at the intruder. He barked and waited to see if the stranger would return. But the old male moved on. Coyote continued hunting for prey.

He walked around a creosote bush studded with yellow flowers and he went by a prickly pear cactus aflame with spring blossoms. He stopped and sniffed the air for his enemy, man, but there was no sign of him. So Coyote trotted along.

Suddenly he perked up his pointed ears with interest. A desert quail was calling from a mesquite stump nearby. He was telling other male quails that he was guarding his territory.

Coyote's heart pounded. A quail would make a good meal for his mate. He crouched low, waiting for the right moment to pounce.

Soon the quail was silent. He hopped from his perch and began feeding on flower seeds scattered on the desert floor. He stopped and looked around for danger, but he did not see Coyote who lay stretched out on the ground now with his eyes half closed. Coyote was playing dead.

The quail moved in Coyote's direction. He ate a few more seeds and then stood still as a statue. He had seen Coyote. Should he fly away? The quail hesitated. Coyote's strange pose puzzled him.

Curious, the quail took one step then another toward Coyote.

Coyote did not move. He held so still that not even his eyes blinked.

This baffled the quail even more. Cocking his head to one side he came closer to investigate.

Coyote saw his chance. He pounced on the quail and killed him.

With his victim dangling from his mouth, Coyote trotted along his favorite runway. Presently he came near his den, an abandoned badger hole that he and his mate had enlarged.

Coyote circled the burrow and sniffed at the wind to see if man was around. He also examined the ground near the den, looking for human footprints. Man would kill his pups if he found them and his mate too.

The coast seemed clear. Coyote went and laid

the dead quail at the entrance to the den. Then he moved on to find food for himself.

Inside the den, the mother coyote lay nursing her pups. She licked their soft, downy fur as they cuddled against her to get more milk. Her ears pricked at the sound of her mate returning. She sniffed the air and caught the scent of the quail, but she waited a few moments before she nudged her cubs aside. Then she cautiously approached the opening of the den. A quick lunge and she had the quail in her mouth.

She was hungry after a long night with her cubs and she tore into the meal her mate had provided. Full, she lay down once more, and her cubs scrambled towards her to finish their breakfast.

2

DRUMMING STATIONS

NOT FAR from Coyote's den a Gila Woodpecker alighted on a giant saguaro cactus. Woodpecker was a handsome bird. His wings were barred in black-and-white and the red patch on his head glistened in the early morning sunlight.

Above him on the saguaro was a hole that a pair of Gila woodpeckers had made for a nest several years ago. It was occupied now by a screech owl. He peered out at Woodpecker and then drew back into the dark cavity.

Woodpecker paid no attention to the owl. He had more important things to do today. Tap! tap! tap! went his bill on the saguaro.

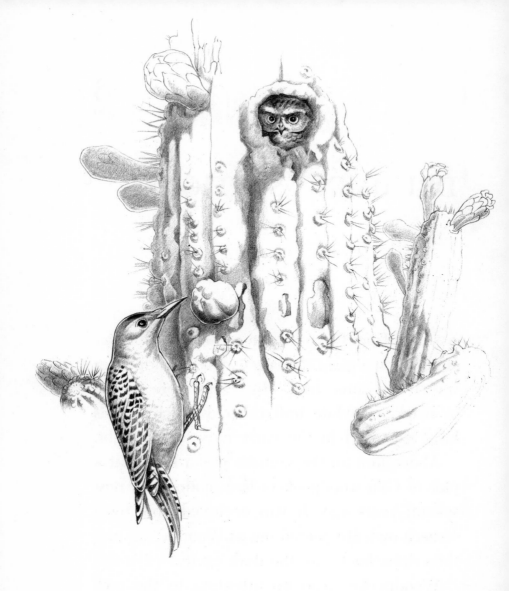

Woodpecker was telling other male woodpeckers that he had staked out his territory and that he would drive a trespasser off his grounds.

For several minutes Woodpecker drummed on the saguaro. Then, uttering a few sharp shrill cries, he flew to another drumming station — the top of a dead mesquite tree.

He tapped some more and was soon answered by a drumming sound from a distance. Another male woodpecker was letting it be known that he was guarding his own territory.

Woodpecker continued on his route. He flew to a nearby paloverde tree, tapped lightly on the bark and listened for insects hiding underneath. He pulled them out and ate them.

Suddenly he saw another male woodpecker about to make a landing on a bush on his territory.

Zoom! Woodpecker dove at the trespasser and stabbed him with his bill.

The stranger took off like a quick moving arrow.

Woodpecker flew to a drumming station and tapped loudly on the tree. He looked to see if the trespasser had returned. There was no sign of him. So Woodpecker drummed some more — this time for a mate.

About a quarter of a mile away another bird was perched upon a high cactus. He was a roadrunner — a long-tailed bird with a spotted topknot, and he could run as fast as 15 miles an hour.

Right now Roadrunner was looking far and wide over his territory. He could easily spot an enemy because he had keen eyesight. It was not long before he saw a trespasser dodge behind a creosote bush.

Roadrunner left his perch in a hurry and streaked along a small open area, leaving a trail of X shaped prints in the sand. He darted in and out among the thorny growth of cacti. Throwing up his long tail, he braked to a stop near the stranger. Then, he chased him off his grounds.

After that Roadrunner returned to the high cactus. He sang a throaty cooing song to warn the stranger and other male roadrunners to stay out of his territory. Then, wishing to attract a mate, he cooed some more, his head rising a little with each note.

For several minutes Roadrunner sang his love song. He stopped and looked around for a hen, but he could not see one anywhere.

Roadrunner was not discouraged, though. He sang some more and enjoyed the morning sun.

Finally, growing hungry, he left his perch and caught a lizard running along the sand. No sooner had he gulped it down than he saw a female roadrunner coming his way.

Roadrunner went to meet her. He strutted in front of the hen. He bowed, raised his head and, with wings drooped and tail spread, cooed in a deep throaty voice.

The hen listened to his song and flipped her long tail with interest. Then she turned and raced across the desert floor.

Roadrunner chased after her. When she stopped by a barrel cactus, he rushed up to her, bowed and cooed again.

This time the hen did not run away. Instead, she and Roadrunner walked off together side by side on his territory.

3

THE DESERT TORTOISE

SEVERAL HOURS had passed since Coyote left the dead quail in front of the den. He had caught a ground squirrel for himself, but now he set off to bring more food to his mate before the hot part of the day when most of the desert animals he hunted would go into hiding.

Coyote trotted across an open area. He stopped to scratch some flea bites, and then looked up at a red-tailed hawk circling high above a saguaro cactus.

A second later the large bird with folded wings dove at great speed. He checked his dive just above the ground and sank his talons into a ground squirrel. Clutching his prey firmly, the

hawk rose into the air and headed for a feeding perch nearby.

Coyote scratched another flea bite and was about to move on when a pair of turkey vultures soaring in the blue sky caught his attention.

With wings outspread the large birds see-sawed in the air. They turned their heads constantly as they glided high over the desert floor hunting for food.

Coyote could not take his eyes away from the vultures. They lived on dead animals and they could spot decayed meat several miles away. Coyote had found some good meals by following them.

Before long the vultures sailed toward an area a short distance from Coyote. They gradually dropped down and gathered over something alongside the road.

Coyote raced along the desert until he caught up with the vultures.

Immediately they took to the air. They were big but they were weak, timid birds and they did not want to fight Coyote. On the ground was a dead badger.

Coyote had a good meal. Then, he cut off a large piece of decayed meat with his back teeth and started to the den with it.

On the way he went by a desert tortoise whose dome-shaped shell protected him from predators.

Tortoise moved slowly and clumsily across the desert floor of his territory. He stopped and ate some wild flowers. He nipped at a prickly pear cactus and was about to eat more when he saw a female tortoise coming toward him. Her shell was larger than his.

Tortoise made his way to the female and started to court her. With neck outstretched, he bobbed his head up and down.

The female withdrew her head and legs into her shell.

Tortoise did not leave. He nudged the female

several times, and he nipped gently on the edge
of her shell.

Just then another male tortoise came up to
the female.

Tortoise bobbed his head up and down in
anger. He had seen the female first and he was
going to fight for her. Besides, the intruder was
on his territory.

Heads withdrawn, Tortoise and the stranger rushed together and pushed with all their might. They separated and looked over the situation. Then they came together again. Standing as high as they could on their broad legs, they nipped each other and pushed some more.

Suddenly Tortoise twisted to one side and flipped the stranger over on his back. Now he had won the fight. He stood and watched quietly.

The loser was helpless. The sun would scorch his underbelly. If he did not right himself, he would die. He jerked one leg in the air. He rocked from side to side. Finally he managed to roll over. Without even glancing at Tortoise he slowly crawled away.

Tortoise went to the female who was waiting nearby. He began to court her again, and after a while they moved along, stopping now and then to munch on tasty wild flowers.

4

THE HOT AFTERNOON

IT WAS MIDAFTERNOON on the desert now. The temperature soared and waves of heat rose up from the sand.

Coyote sat in the shade under the branches of a desert shrub to wait out the hot part of the day. From his retreat he kept watch on the den and his surroundings, ready to spring into action if he caught the scent of danger.

In different parts of the desert, other animals were also avoiding the midday heat. Tortoise and his mate had crawled into separate shallow holes. A sidewinder, or horned rattlesnake, lay coiled in a deserted ground squirrel burrow — the direct sun would kill the snake in a short time. A kangaroo rat plugged the entrance to its underground den to keep in moisture and cool air. And a jackrabbit stayed in a small hollow shaded by grasses.

Only a few lizards ran across open spaces, their bodies raised so as not to touch the sun-baked sand. One was the desert iguana, or crested lizard. He was a handsome creature with a cream-colored body marked with reddish-brown spots and a long tail. He looked like a miniature dragon.

Iguana was scampering on his territory, searching for food. He stopped and ate some

creosote flowers. Then he sniffed for scent trails left by male iguanas.

He could not find any, so he ran upright, flicking his long tail for balance. From this position he could tell better if there were trespassers on his feeding grounds. But all he saw were shrubs, a few prickly pear cacti and some giant saguaros.

Presently Iguana paused in the shade of a rock not far from where Coyote was resting. He did not see his enemy whose yellowish-gray fur blended with the surroundings. Neither did he

catch his scent since the wind was blowing in the other direction.

With his back turned to Coyote, Iguana also rested. Not for long, though. Suddenly, Coyote sprang forward and grabbed him by the tail.

Quick as a flash Iguana twisted to one side. Snap! Off came his long tail. Iguana scooted away, leaving Coyote still looking at the squirming tail he held in his teeth.

In time Iguana would grow a new tail. It would not be as perfect as the old one, but at least he would have a tail.

Coyote ate the detachable tail and then returned to the cover of the desert shrub.

He rested his head on his paws and watched an ant hill, a mound of sand that harvester ants had piled up when digging their den. Many of the ants had gone underground, but a few still braved the heat. They were cutting seeds off from grasses and taking them to their nest.

Coyote was tired and he began to doze. At a rustling sound he opened one eye and saw Roadrunner near the ant hill. But Coyote was too full and sleepy to move. His eyes closed again.

Roadrunner moved closer to the ant hill. He did not mind when the temperatures soared because his feathers insulated him from the heat of the sun. He snatched up several ants in his bill and ate them. Then he stood very still. There was a rattlesnake lying partly coiled in the shade of a rock a few yards away. The reptile was not large, so Roadrunner felt he could tackle him.

He walked slowly toward his prey, waving his long tail from side to side. As he drew close, the rattlesnake coiled, ready to attack with his fangs.

Roadrunner darted in at the snake but moved quickly back to escape his deadly thrust.

The angry reptile struck again. Once more

Roadrunner skillfully dodged his fangs. He darted forward again and again until the snake was so tired that he was off guard for a second.

Roadrunner quickly danced in and grasped the snake's head in his long bill. He thrashed the reptile's head on a rock and killed him. Then he began gulping him down head-first.

But the snake proved to be more than Roadrunner could digest at once. So he scuttled along the sand with the tail dangling from his bill.

As Roadrunner disappeared around a desert bush, Coyote got up, stretching one leg then the other. But he made no move to go out into the hot sun. Instead, he listened to the wind stirring the cacti and desert shrubs.

Before long the wind started to blow hard. It picked up loose sand and debris on the desert floor. It swept them along, past Coyote's resting place and carried them up into the air like a spinning top.

Coyote watched the dust devil, or small whirlwind, until it disappeared like smoke into the air. Then he lowered his head and dozed again.

5

THE
CHUCKWALLA LIZARD

THE SUN was setting beyond the mountains in the west, and the desert was painted a golden glow. As the colors deepened in the sky, birds started singing their evening songs.

A thrasher whistled a clear "whit-wheet" from a mesquite tree. A vermillion flycatcher rose into the air and sang a cheerful tune. And Woodpecker tapped on a saguaro cactus.

Not far from Woodpecker's territory several quail moved slowly toward one of the few water holes left from the winter rains. On the way they stopped and pecked at some seeds, watching for signs of danger as they ate.

Finally the procession of quail reached the watering place. While one acted as lookout, the others dipped their bills into the water and drank thirstily.

The quails did not stay long. Many predators visited the water hole, so animals did not linger there. Only a few creatures never had to make the dangerous trip to the drinking place. They got enough water to survive from the moisture stored in the plants and animals they ate.

Before long Roadrunner appeared at the water hole. Then came a bobcat, an animal that was greatly feared on the desert. The quails flew away, but Roadrunner just kept a safe distance from the bobcat, who drank quietly and left. When a five-foot rattlesnake arrived, Roadrunner did not attack it. He was still full from his last meal. The snake sucked up water and then went back the way it came.

Coyote came for his drink too. Roadrunner had left and in his place was a broad-striped skunk.

Coyote avoided going near the skunk. He lapped up some water and then moved slowly

along, hunting up wind so that the scent of prey would be carried to him.

Presently he came near a horned lizard. His back and head were edged with sharp horn-like spines, and his color blended into the stretches of desert sand.

Horned Lizard had been active during the day, feeding on ants and other insects that he snapped up with his sticky tongue. Now he was about to bury himself in the sand where he would be warm when it grew cold during the night, and where he would be safe from predators.

Horned Lizard scurried past a rock and reached an area of loose soil.

Just then he caught sight of Coyote a few yards away.

Terrified, Horned Lizard plunged head-first into the sand. He wriggled and squirmed into the desert floor until not an inch of him showed. He waited with rapidly beating heart.

Coyote could dig the lizard out, but he did not disturb the cover of sand. He knew from experience that the sharp spines of a horned lizard would hurt his throat if he tried to eat him.

Coyote moved on, searching for other prey. Before long he came within a short distance of another lizard who was about to go into hiding for the night. He was a chuckwalla, a large plump reptile who liked to eat the buds, leaves and flowers of desert plants.

During the day Chuckwalla had patrolled his territory, looking for other male chuckwallas. He had also searched for a mate, but had not found one.

Chuckwalla nibbled on a cactus flower. He was unaware that Coyote was moving quietly in his direction. He kept on eating and enjoying his meal.

Suddenly a noise made him turn in alarm. Coyote had stepped on a fallen mesquite twig.

Instantly Chuckwalla went into action. He scooted to some rocks on the dry slope of his home range. He crawled into a crevice. He sucked up air and blew himself up like a balloon.

Coyote rushed up to the rock crevice. He tried to get hold of Chuckwalla and pull him out, but he could not budge the lizard because he was twice his normal size.

Coyote growled. He tried once more to dislodge Chuckwalla, but he still was unable to remove the lizard from the rock crevice. Finally Coyote wandered off to look for easier prey to catch.

6

THE RATTLESNAKE

Twilight shadows gathered over the desert and a cool breeze tossed the wild flowers to and fro.

Many creatures who hunted during the day were hidden away for the night. Woodpecker and Roadrunner, with heads tucked under their wings, were asleep on their roosting places. Tortoise dozed in a shallow burrow. Iguana and other lizards had also gone underground.

Coyote was still on the prowl for prey since many night animals had left their dens and burrows to hunt in the cool of the evening. A jackrabbit ran along one of his favorite trails. Overhead a bat flew here and there snatching insects on the wing. And a six-foot diamondback rattlesnake glided slowly along with his head slightly raised.

Rattlesnake soon disappeared in the underbrush, but in a little while he came out into the open. He flicked his forked tongue to test the air for odors and for scent trails left by other rattlesnakes. He kept crawling slowly, his long body forming huge S shaped marks in the sand.

Soon he came upon a trail made by a female rattlesnake. The scent was freshly made and led Rattlesnake to a group of beavertail cacti. Here he found the female, her pale coloring and diamond-shaped spots nearly matching his own.

Rattlesnake moved closer to the female, his forked tongue darting in and out as he touched her.

The female made no effort to move on.

Just then another rattlesnake slithered around the cacti. He was a male diamondback.

The rivals lifted their heads and necks into the air, ready to wrestle each other. With bodies

entwined, the male snakes pressed their heads
together and pushed for all they were worth.
They swayed back and forth, each one trying
to force the other to the ground.

They separated and came together again. This time Rattlesnake used all his strength. He pushed very hard and pinned his rival's head on the desert floor.

Now that he was the victor, Rattlesnake released the stranger and watched him disappear among the twilight shadows.

Then Rattlesnake returned to look for the female who had been watching the fight. But she was nowhere to be seen. Rattlesnake glided away, his forked tongue flicking the air for a scent trail that would lead him to a mate.

It was not long before he came to an abrupt stop. A broad-striped skunk came up and walked directly in front of him.

Immediately Rattlesnake coiled. He buzzed his rattles loudly.

A rabbit out hunting nearby scurried for cover at the sound of the snake's rattles, but not the skunk. He ambled along, unafraid. He had his own powerful weapon of defense — his bad odor.

Rattlesnake buzzed some more and then uncoiled himself. Even he would not attack the

skunk. He sampled the air with his forked
tongue. He crawled past some wild flowers on
his territory and around a log on the desert floor.

Suddenly Rattlesnake stopped short. Two
small pits on his face had sensed the heat of a
small warm-blooded animal. It was a pocket
mouse.

Rattles silent, the huge snake slithered after
the mouse who was so busy eating that he did
not see him.

With a lightning-quick strike Rattlesnake in-
jected venom from his fangs, or needle-like hollow teeth, into the flesh of his prey.

The mouse died quickly, and Rattlesnake
swallowed him whole. Then he crawled to a
barrel cactus and lay alongside it to digest his
food.

7

THE KANGAROO RAT

A FULL MOON shone in a sky studded with thousands of stars.

On the desert, insects called walking sticks fed on the foliage. Moths settled on evening primroses and then flew on. And animals searched for food.

Cautiously, a kangaroo rat came out of his underground burrow. He had spent the hot daylight hours there. He even plugged the burrow opening with dirt to keep heat out and moisture in. Now he moved carefully, avoiding the bright moonlit places where he would be an easy target for enemies.

Kangaroo Rat was one of the most hunted creatures on the desert. He stood only five inches high but coyotes, bobcats, owls and other predators were always on the lookout for him. That was because his body contained a lot of moisture and water was scarce on the dry desert.

Kangaroo Rat stood erect and tense, his dark bright eyes taking in everything around him. All seemed safe. With a flick of his long tail and his tiny forefeet clasped under his chin, he bounded off with great springing leaps.

He found a large moonlight shadow made by a desert shrub. Kangaroo Rat paused to groom himself. He rubbed oil from a gland on his back through his cream-colored fur. He rolled in the sand to remove the excess oil so that his fur would not mat and become sticky. Then he shook himself from his head to the end of his long tail tipped with a brush. His fur was soft and fluffy now.

Kangaroo Rat was ready to go seed hunting, but first he looked for signs of predators. Finding that the coast was clear, he bounded across an open stretch of sand in the moonlight and into the dark shadows along a familiar trail.

When he came to a creosote bush, he rubbed a scent pad between his shoulders against it.

He left a waxy substance as a warning signal to other kangaroo rats to stay out of his territory.

After that Kangaroo Rat was busy collecting seeds. Using his tiny paws he gathered them from grasses and stuffed them in his large cheek pouches.

Kangaroo Rat spent many hours storing seeds in a chamber in his burrow. He could live his whole lifetime without ever going to the water-hole to drink. He got all the water he needed from these desert seeds.

He crammed more in his cheek pouches and then, hopping along on his hind legs like a kangaroo, headed for home.

As he came near his burrow, he saw a strange form close to the entrance. It was another kangaroo rat, his cheeks puffed out with seeds that he had stolen from the owner's storage room.

Kangaroo Rat dashed up to the thief. They seemed to size each other up like boxers before a fight. They came together and pushed and clawed with their forepaws.

Then they separated to get their breaths and glared at each other.

A few moments later they rushed together

again. This time they leaped high in the air and kicked each other with their long hind legs. Sand flew in all directions.

This did not stop the two from fighting. They rolled on the desert floor. They nipped at each other's fur with their sharp teeth.

But Kangaroo Rat was quicker than his opponent. He bit him on the tail.

Squeaking in pain, the thief managed to beat a hasty retreat.

Kangaroo chased him a short way and then went back to his burrow. He hurried down to his storage room. He found that the thief had taken many seeds. His fur bristling, Kangaroo Rat went outside.

Nose quivering, he sniffed the air for the dreaded scent of an enemy. Deciding that it was safe to go about his business, he bounded over to his foraging grounds.

He worked fast with his paws gathering seeds and stuffing them in his cheek pouches. He even used the claws on his hind feet to sift through the sand for buried seeds.

With a full load Kangaroo Rat headed for home.

8

THE STRANGE SCENT

TIME SLIPPED BY. The moon still shone on the desert, turning the sand into glimmering sheets of silver.

A cold breeze flowed down from the mountains, but the day animals were snug and warm in their burrows and hiding places.

The night animals did not mind the drop in temperature. They preferred the cool night. Their one concern was to find food.

Coyote had been on the prowl for hours. Now he cut across his territory, a catch for his mate grasped firmly in his mouth. On his way, he paused by a paloverde tree and left a fresh scent on its trunk. He was near his den and

wanted to leave a warning for strangers. Then, he stopped short. There was a strange scent on the night breeze. He dropped his catch and sniffed the ground. There, circling close to his den, were the footprints of his dreaded enemy — man.

Coyote headed for the shadow of a desert shrub, his heart pounding. From his hiding place he would watch and listen for man's return. As he crouched silently in the darkness, his sharp ears picked up a whimpering noise. Cautiously, Coyote left the cover of the bush and approached his den. Just outside the opening he stopped and sniffed the ground and listened. The soft crying was louder now. Coyote peered inside. There alone in the darkness, sat one tiny pup. It was whining softly and nosing the ground.

Coyote's mate was nowhere in sight. Neither were the other young ones.

Coyote nuzzled his frightened pup and quieted the small one's cries. Then he sniffed the floor. The scent of his mate led out of the den. Coyote followed it into the moonlit night and

scanned the desert horizon. There, in the distance he saw her. She trotted up to him and they touched noses. Then mother coyote entered the den. She licked the furry pup and picked it up in her teeth. Holding it by the loose skin on the back of its neck, she trotted outside.

Coyote followed his mate and together they crossed the desert to a distant corner of his territory. Mother coyote had moved her litter to another den, one that was far from the scent of man.

Once inside the new den, mother coyote

gently placed the last pup with the rest of her family. Her young ones clambered over each other in their rush to be near their mother.

But Coyote stayed outside the den. He stretched out in front of the entrance and watched the desert horizon. After a rest he would go out into the night to hunt for a meal for his mate.

In another part of the desert a gecko lizard was looking for food. Gecko was a small slender lizard with a large head and a short tail. He was yellow in color with brown crossbands, and he liked to eat tiny beetles and other small prey.

Gecko scooted on padless toes across an open area of his territory. As he drew near a rock he came to an abrupt stop. Then, like a cat stalking a mouse, Gecko moved quietly toward a small beetle, bright and shiny in the moonlight. He pounced upon the little creature, killed it and had a meal.

Still being cautious, he scurried across another open space. He was about to look for more beetles when his cat-like eyes caught a movement. There was another gecko lizard, making its way around a desert shrub.

Gecko was ready to fight this stranger on his territory. He raised himself a few inches off the ground. With his back arched, he puffed out his throat and with lowered head circled the male. He bumped him several times. Then, squeaking as he rushed forward, Gecko bit the intruder on the snout.

The invading gecko squeaked in pain. He darted off, but he did not get very far. A screech owl dropped low, grabbed the lizard in his talons and flew away with him.

Gecko saw what happened, and scooted to safety under a rock. He waited there until the danger passed.

9

THE JACKRABBIT

A BLACK-TAILED jackrabbit also saw the screech owl fly off with the gecko lizard. Immediately she looked toward her nest where three young jackrabbits were hidden. Had one of them ventured out into the open and become easy prey for the screech owl?

Jackrabbit bounded along a worn trail and soon came to her nest that was hollowed out in a clump of grass. She found her three babies all together, snug and warm. They had been born a few days ago with brownish-gray fur and bright wide open eyes.

Jackrabbit nursed her babies. Then she covered them with grass and left the nest to get food for herself. She nibbled on the leaves from low hanging mesquite branches, but she was always on the alert. She watched for the swooping forms of eagles and hawks and the prowling shapes of bobcats, coyotes and foxes.

Jackrabbit also watched for other jackrabbits. Like many desert animals, she had a territory.

Her way of warning trespassers away from her feeding ground was to leave droppings at certain spots.

Right now, she deposited some droppings in a neat pile alongside a creosote bush and then moved on to a barrel cactus. Carefully, she pushed her nose between the spines and used her teeth to pull a piece of cactus loose. The water in the cactus helped jackrabbit survive on the dry hot desert.

While feeding, she twitched her ears in all directions. Her eyes scanned the ground and the sky. Her sight was so sharp she could cover the entire area with one quick glance.

In the distance, she heard the screech owl's mournful wail. He was announcing to other screech owls in the vicinity that he had staked out his territory. Jackrabbit kept a watchful eye on her nest.

After a while she perked up her huge ears in alarm. Another sound filled the air, a rustling sound that told her an animal was prowling close by.

Just then the wind changed and brought a strong scent. Jackrabbit recognized the odor at once. It came from Coyote. He was on her trail.

Ears flattened back, Jackrabbit bounded away in a race for her life. She leaped past a group of cacti. She dashed on at full speed — 15 feet at a bound, four bounds in a second.

Coyote, eyes glittering with hunger, chased after her.

Jackrabbit could feel him gaining, but she did not slacken her speed. She headed along a familiar trail that circled her range.

Coyote kept following her, but after a while he began losing speed. Usually, he hunted with his mate. When he tired during a chase, she would relieve him. With her help they always succeeded in catching a jackrabbit. But now his mate was nursing and taking care of their young.

Coyote was not going to give up this chase, though. He ran some more, his tail waving behind him like a plume. Jackrabbit ran hard and fast, bounding over shrubs in her way.

The many trails she had worn criss-crossed each other. She switched quickly from one to the next, leaving her pursuer farther and farther behind. Finally she swerved onto a trail that led to the edge of her territory. She stopped and hid in a hollow under a bush.

Coyote sniffed along one trail. He dashed back and picked up another trail and still another. By this time he was so confused that he did not know which way to turn. Growling in anger he left for other hunting grounds.

Finally Jackrabbit peeped out of her hiding place. She wanted to find out if Coyote had found her nest. She hopped along quietly, following the shadows all the way.

At last she reached her nest. Three tiny jackrabbits were asleep under the blanket of grass. Jackrabbit lay down beside them to rest after her experience with Coyote.

Coyote was moving slowly across an open area now. Soon he picked up the scent of a pocket mouse. He crept forward and pounced upon the little creature. After killing it, he ate the mouse hungrily. Then, hiding in some brush along the trail of a rabbit, he pounced upon the cottontail as soon as it came by. But this catch he decided to take back to his mate.

With his victim dangling from his mouth, Coyote trotted to the den. As he laid the dead cottontail at the entrance, his mate came out and they touched noses.

Coyote looked into the den. In the darkness he saw four small coyotes, their eyes tightly shut. His pups were fast asleep. Coyote turned and disappeared into the shadows to look for more prey.

Soon he caught another cottontail and had a good meal. Then he lay down under the low branches of a mesquite tree and slept lightly in snatches always listening for danger.

When he finally got up, the rosy light of dawn shone in the east, and the cacti and wild flowers were bathed in scarlet and gold.

Coyote stretched his legs. Throwing back his head, he looked up at the sky and howled his early morning song to greet another day on the desert.

BIBLIOGRAPHY

Barker, Will: *Familiar Reptiles & Amphibians of America,* New York, Harper & Row Pub., 1964.

Cahalane, Victor H.: *Mammals of North America,* New York, MacMillan Co., 1947.

Carr, Marion B.: *Roadrunners,* Nature and Science Magazine, May 1, 1964, New York, Natural History Press.

Carrighar, Sally: *Wild Heritage,* Boston, Houghton, 1965.

Carthy, J. D.: *Animals and Their Ways,* Garden City, New York, Natural History Press, 1965.

Eibl-Eibesfeldt: *Fighting Behavior of Animals,* Scientific American Magazine, December 1961, Scientific American Inc.

Freedman, Russel & Morris, James E.: *Animal Instincts,* New York, Holiday House, Inc., 1970.

Goodheart, Barbara: *A Year On The Desert,* Englewood Cliffs, New Jersey, Prentice-Hall Inc., 1969.

Klots, Alexander B. & Klots, Elsie B.: *The Desert,* Mankato, Minnesota, Creative Educational Soc., 1967.

Leopold A. Starker: *The Desert,* New York, Time Inc., 1961.

Mykytowyez, R.: *Territorial Markings By Rabbits,* Scientific American, May 1968, New York, Scientific American Inc.

National Audubon Society: *The Audubon Nature Encyclopedia,* Philadelphia, New York, Curtis Pub. Co., 1964.

Norman, James: *The Strange World of Reptiles,* New York, G. P. Putnam's Sons, 1966.

Olin, George: *Mammals of the Southwest Deserts,* Globe, Arizona, Southwestern Monuments Assoc., 1954.

Pettit, Ted S.: *Animal Signs and Signals,* Garden City, New York, Doubleday & Co., Inc., 1961.

Seton, Ernest Thompson: *Lives of Game Animals,* Volume I, Garden City, New York, Doubleday Doran & Co., 1925.

Sutton, Anne & Myron, *Life of the Desert,* New York, McGraw-Hill Book Co., 1966.

The American Museum of Natural History: *The Illustrated Encyclopedia of Animal Life,* New York, Greystone, 1961.

Van Wormer, Joe: *The World of the Coyote,* Philadelphia, New York, J. B. Lippincott Co., 1964.

INDEX

MARY ADRIAN

Born in Sewickley, Pennsylvania, Mary Adrian now lives in Portland, Oregon. She and her husband, Henry Jorgensen, are both members of the National Audubon Society and the National Wildlife Federation. Mary Adrian is the author of a wide range of books about nature and conservation for young readers:

Nature Mysteries

The Ghost Town Mystery
The Lightship Mystery
The Kite Mystery
The Indian Horse Mystery
The Mystery of the Dinosaur Bones
The Skin Diving Mystery
The Mystery of the Night Explorers
The Rare Stamp Mystery
The Fox Hollow Mystery
The Uranium Mystery

The Preserve Our Wildlife Series

The American Eagle
The American Mustang
The North American Wolf
The North American Bighorn Sheep
The American Alligator
The American Prairie Chicken

The Balance of Nature Series

A Day and A Night In A Forest
A Day and A Night In the Arctic
A Day and A Night in a Tidepool

JEAN ZALLINGER

A well-known nature artist, Mrs. Zallinger has drawn practically every kind of animal, living or extinct. Besides a number of children's science books, her work has appeared in magazines, encyclopedias, medical journals and text books.

The mother of three grown children, Mrs. Zallinger now lives in North Haven, Connecticut, with her husband, Rudolph, who is also an artist.